ntroduction

So, you're putting on a Messianic Passover *seder*. You get the applause if everything goes smoothly. And if it *doesn't*...well...but don't even think about that. Of *course* it will go smoothly. We're helping you, right? Right!

A friend of ours has a catchy way to describe the principles of management. She says, "We recruit, educate, motivate, and delegate!" It has a certain ring, doesn't it? Keep this in mind as you prepare your Messianic Passover *seder*.

Whether you are having a table-full, a room-full, or a social hall-full of people for this beautiful, meaningful experience, it is essential to get your helpers *recruited, educated, motivated* and *delegated.*

1. Recruiting

You probably already know the people you can approach and count on for help. For a small family *seder* this may not be more than one helper. But for an entire congregation, "the more the merrier." Call together your group of volunteers for a meeting after services or at someone's home over dessert. (That will keep you from getting hungry as you discuss the delicious Passover menu.)

2. Educating

Why not begin by sitting down with *The Messianic Passover Haggadah* and treating yourself and your helpers to a little preview of the event to come? It might be easier to attack the task of preparing for Passover when the meaning of that preparation is understood. Working toward a goal can be much more pleasant when everyone can envision and understand that goal.

3. Motivating

Some of the instructions in our guide need to be strictly followed. For example, the Bible is very clear to say that leavened products are off-limits at Passover. Also, we have suggested two alternative menus. Think of it as something from Column A and something from Column B. Choosing the menu ought to be helpful in motivating your recruits. And sharing with them the joy people will receive from participating in the *seder* will be motivational as well.

4. Delegating

This is most important of all. Don't assume the entire burden of this project. Some of your volunteers will be food preparers, some setter-uppers, some servers, and some cleaner-uppers. Decide in advance what part you wish to play in this procedure and be sure to delegate the rest. Remember, you are the conductor, *not* the entire orchestra!

A Word About Words

Although Passover is traditionally a Jewish holiday, we are delighted to find more and more gentiles discovering the significance of the Festival of Redemption. Since *The Messianic Passover Haggadah* contains some Hebrew words that may be unfamiliar to some preparing for the *seder*, (like *"seder,"* for instance!), we have prepared a glossary of Hebrew words to help. We list them in the order that they appear in *The Messianic Passover Haggadah*. You won't need to *memorize* the list! Just read it over if you are not yet familiar with Passover. You may want to refer to the pronunciation guide in the front of this book

Messianic	Pertaining to the Messiah
Haggadah	The telling; the book narrating the Passover
Seder	Order; the order of the Passover service
Khameytz	Leaven; any items made with yeast
Bedikat Khameytz	The search for the leaven
Yeshua	Hebrew for "Jesus"
Kadeysh	Sanctification; the cup of sanctification
Urkhatz	The hand-washing ceremony
Karpas	Greens; usually parsley, sometimes lettuce
Ma Nishtanah	"How different"; the four questions asked by a young child at Passover
Matzah	Unleavened bread
Matzot	Plural for *matzah*

Afikomen	This is actually not Hebrew, but Greek. It means "the coming one," and is the name given to a special piece of broken *matzah*
Maror	Bitter herbs (preferably red, grated horseradish)
Kharoset	apple-based mixture symbolizing mortar, or clay (recipe included)
Maggid	The narration of the Passover story from the book of Exodus
Pesach	Passover; also, the Paschal lamb
Khagigah	A special name given to the roasted egg on the *seder* plate, symbolizing the Temple sacrifice
Dayenu	"It would have been sufficient"; a popular Passover song by the same name (included later)
Torah	The five books of Moses; the Pentateuch
Shulkhan Oreykh	The Passover meal
Tzafun	The ceremony of bringing back the *afikomen*
Eliyahu HaNavi	Elijah the Prophet; a popular Passover song by the same name (included later)
Hallel	Praise; Psalm 136, called the "Great Hallel," is included in the *Haggadah*
Lashanah Haba'a bi Yerushalayim	"Next Year in Jerusalem!" — a traditional wish expressed at the conclusion of the Passover *seder*; a popular Passover song of the same name (included later)

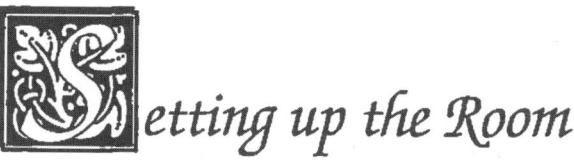 etting up the Room

Although this guide will apply to all sizes of Messianic Passover *seders*, we will speak as if addressing those responsible for a larger group. If you are having a small family gathering, you will find what you need, too.

For those setting up many tables in a social hall or community room, you will have to let the room guide you in your decisions concerning set-up. Bear in mind that one person will be the main leader, narrating much of the Messianic Passover *seder*. Be sure he or she is situated at a table so as to be seen and heard throughout the room.

Because Passover is a family holiday, we suggest keeping families together. Each table should have a "mama" and a "papa" (these can be an actual mother and father, or can be assigned roles.) Mamas sit at one end and Papas at the other. Two candlesticks with white candles and matches should be set in front of the mama's place; the plate containing the three *matzot* (see item #4 on page 8) should be near the papa. The papa will be the main leader, breaking the *matzah* and hiding it (this will be explained in greater detail later), passing the bowl of water for hand-washing, and fulfilling other such functions.

 *etting the Table*

Besides chairs, plates, silverware (or plastic-ware), drink-cups and the usual dinner items, there are certain other items essential for Passover.

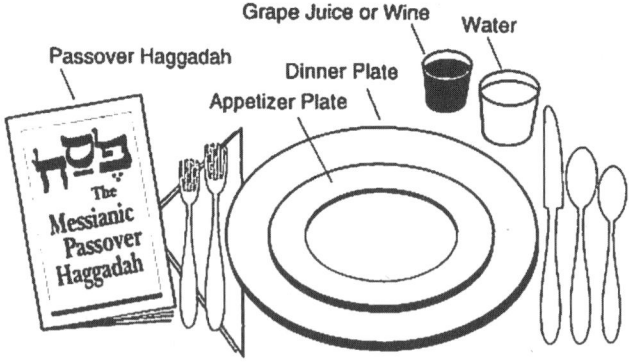

6

1. Elijah's Place

As you plan your table arrangements reserve a seat and a place-setting for Elijah the Prophet. If you are having many tables, do this at the head table. Maybe you weren't expecting Elijah, but it *is* a Passover tradition to do so. It will be explained later.

2. Wine Cups

In addition to cups for water or other beverages to be drunk during the meal, you will need to have a special cup for the fruit of the vine at each place. This cup is filled and drunk from four times during the *seder*.

3. The Seder Plate

The illustration below will help you set-up your *seder* plate. Each table will require its own *seder* plate with enough of each item to be shared. You can purchase a decorated *seder* plate or simply use a plain dinner plate. A cupful of ground or grated (not creamed) horseradish should do nicely; a cupful of *kharoset* (apple mixture) should also suffice. You will need as many sprigs of parsley as you have place settings. A single egg is fine; one horseradish root (or onion, if you can't find a horseradish root) will do, since it is not actually eaten. One cup of salt water can be passed around the table, too. You will also need a small bowl or basin of water and extra napkins for handwashing.

7

4. Matzah

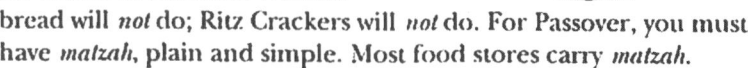

This is a must; there is no substitute for *matzah* at Passover. Wonder bread will *not* do; Ritz Crackers will *not* do. For Passover, you must have *matzah*, plain and simple. Most food stores carry *matzah*.

On each table, you'll need a *matzah tash*. This is the *matzah* "unity," as described on page 13 of the *haggadah*. You can buy a beautiful matzah tash or construct one as follows: begin by placing a completely opened napkin on a plate. Place a whole sheet of *matzah* upon it. Next, another open napkin. Then another sheet of *matzah*. Continue layering that way until you've used three pieces of *matzah* and four napkins.

During the *seder*, the leader at the table will reach into this *matzah* "unity" and remove the middle piece. After it is broken, he will wrap it in another napkin, which you should set aside for that purpose, or you can use the *afikomen* bag that is supplied with some *matzah tashes*. One last thing about *matzah*. Include a separate plate stacked with sheets (no napkins this time) of *matzah* for eating during the meal! (Figure one or two pieces per person.)

5. Pillows

Since we are instructed to recline during the Passover *seder*, you may ask participants to bring a pillow from home to place behind them on their seats.

6. Shankbone of a Lamb

This last item will require a trip to the butcher. This bone is the last of the ceremonial elements for the *seder* plate. The shankbone must be unbroken. If you wash it well and roast the bone in the oven for a bit it keeps nicely. You can use it each year for Passover.

ansoming the Afikomen

The game that has become connected with the piece of

matzah known as the *afikomen* (*The Messianic Passover Haggadah*, pages 13 and 27) has helped tailor the Passover holiday to the children. Whereas every family has embellished the tradition surrounding this disappearing and reappearing piece of *matzah*, there seem to be two basic ways to play the game.

In the first variation, the papa asks the children to cover their eyes so that he may hide the wrapped *afikomen* from them. After the meal, a few minutes are devoted to searching for the afikomen; when it is found the leader "pays" for its return.

In the second version of the game, the leader sets the *afikomen* on the table where he is seated. The object of the game then is for the children to "steal" the treasure from him during the course of the meal when he is looking elsewhere. The ransoming then takes place after the meal as the *seder* service resumes.

(*Afikomen* prices have risen along with food, real estate and everything else, and the *afikomen* is often ransomed for as much as a dollar. Let the reader be warned.)

Afikomen, as we have explained, means "the coming one." The ransoming game draws the children's attention back to the *seder*, and back to the *afikomen*. From there the serious matter of God's redemption is discussed. At this point it would be most appropriate to discuss, or even participate in the bread and wine ceremony instituted by Yeshua (Jesus) at his last supper.

ur Wish for You

We are certain that your Messianic Passover *seder* will be a time of spiritual refreshment and a good deal of fun, too. And since it was God's idea that the holiday be celebrated with a *feast*,

A Blessed Passover in the Messiah!

Barry Rubin

Enough Talk...
Let's Get Cooking!
— or —
Passover Recipes Like Mama Used to Make
(well, at least like *my* Mama)

If you or those in your congregation have never tasted Jewish food, don't worry. You actually have a certain advantage — no one will complain, "It sure doesn't taste like Mama used to make!" Take heart, you'll do fine.

So even if your mama didn't make Passover when you grew up, there's no time like the present to start yourself a whole new family tradition. Then, when your children are grown they can complain with pride: "It sure doesn't taste like Mama used to make!" It never does. *We wish you a sweet Pesach in the Messiah!*

First, let me give you the recipe for *kharoset*, that apple-mixture used during the ceremonial part of the Passover *seder*. Although it represents mortar, it really does not contain concrete, sand or straw. It is, rather, a delicious mixture that has always been a favorite at Passover and can be eaten *during the meal* as well as ceremonially (so be sure and make extra!)

KHAROSET
1/2 cup walnuts ground up fine
1 nice, tart apple (estimate 1/4 apple per person)
1 Tbls. Passover wine, or grape juice
1 tsp. sugar or honey
1/2 tsp. cinnamon
optional: nutmeg or cloves, raisins

Pare, core, peel, and grate the apple; add the rest and leave it all in the refrigerator for several hours, allowing it to turn brown. (Yes, it's *supposed* to turn brown. Trust me.)

Menus to Choose From

Below are two sample menus for Passover. One features meat as a main dish, the other, poultry. You can mix and match, as we said. The dishes for which recipes have been provided are numbered.

COLUMN A	COLUMN B
Gefilte Fish on a Leaf of Lettuce*	Tossed Green Salad
Chicken Soup[1] with *Matzah* Ball[2]	Chicken Soup[1] with *Matzah* Ball[2] (no choice here)
Brisket[3] (or other roasted meat)	Roast Chicken (or other poultry)
Matzah Kugel[4]	*Matzah* Stuffing[5]
Carrot Tzimmes[6]	Honeyed Carrots
Fresh Fruit	Applesauce
Sponge Cake[7]	Macaroons (or other Passover cookies)
Coffee/Tea	Coffee/Tea

What? You never heard of gefilte fish? OK. OK. This is something you can buy in the Jewish food section of your supermarket; I would give you the recipe, but believe me, we're talking about a lot of tsuris *(trouble) to make gefilte fish.*

Buy it in the jar, serve one piece per person, and you'll find it'll go beautifully with all that extra horseradish you have leftover from the Passover ceremony.

11

Recipes

1. CHICKEN SOUP
Start with a 4–5 pound chicken, or use the backs and the insides of the chickens you might be serving.

3 quarts of water	2 onions
3 carrots	2 pieces of celery, stalks and tops
1 Tbls. salt	garlic powder: several shakes
1/8 tsp pepper	1/2 tsp. dill weed

Clean the chicken thoroughly; clean and cut up the vegetables. Add all of the ingredients to the water and bring to a boil. Then lower the heat. Simmer for 2 hours. Pour the soup through a colander, and refrigerate broth for 2–3 hours, until the fat forms a layer at the top. Save the carrots and put them aside. Remove the layer of fat and return the broth and carrots to the pot to reheat.

This will boil down to about 2 or 2-1/2 quarts of soup. If you want to stretch it a little, add more water and a few chicken bouillon cubes (when no one is looking).

2. MATZAH BALLS (a.k.a. *Knaidlekh*)
1 cup *matzah* meal (from the Jewish food section in grocery)
1/2 cup water
1/3 cup vegetable oil (this is the healthiest version I know of!)
4 eggs (well, maybe not *that* healthy)
1 tsp. salt
Dash of pepper

Traditionally, matzah balls are made with "schmaltz," rendered chicken fat. But I could not in good conscience recommend such an artery-clogger in this day and age.
Better you should use some nice polyunsaturated oil.
I promise, the matzah balls will still be light and fluffy. Trust me.

Beat the eggs. Add water, oil, salt and pepper to the eggs; mix well. Add the *matzah* meal and stir thoroughly. Refrigerate for one hour. (See, you *should* have read this before you started!)

Bring a pot of slightly salted water to a rolling boil. Form the *matzah* meal mixture into golf-ball size balls and drop (gently, please) into the water. First they sink, but then they should rise to the top. If yours don't they will be called "*matzah* bombs."

Cook 20 minutes. You may set these aside and later add them to the soup, before serving. Makes about 12 *matzah* balls.

3. BRISKET

This particular recipe recommends overnight marinating and four hours of roasting. You may substitute some other roasted beef if you wish. (If you're even *thinking* about a pork roast, forget it—you've got the wrong holiday.)

5 lb. piece of brisket (or other meat)
2 onions
2 carrots (nice, thin slices)

Marinade:
>   1/3 cup lemon juice   1 tsp. salt
>   1/3 cup oil   1 tsp. sugar or honey
>   1/4 cup tarragon (or other flavor) vinegar
>   Several hefty shakes of garlic powder, or 6 sliced garlic cloves

Make the marinade first; then peel and slice the vegetables. Set the brisket and vegetables in a shallow roasting pan and pour on the marinade, coating the meat all over as though you were rinsing off a baby. Cover the pan with aluminum foil and refrigerate overnight. When you think of it the following day, turn the meat over.

Five hours before dinner time, set the pan, still covered tightly, in a 350° oven. Roast for 4 to 4-1/2 hours, until fork-tender. Let the meat sit out for awhile after cooking to cool, which will make it easier to cut. (Try taking it out of the oven as the *seder* begins.) Cut the brisket across the grain and pour the reheated marinade and vegetables over the meat before serving. (Believe me, you'll never miss the pork roast!) Serves 15–20.

4. MATZAH KUGEL
3 pieces of matzah
1/2 cup seedless raisins
6 eggs
4 grated apples (tart ones are best!)
1/2 cup sugar
grated rind of 1 orange
1/4 cinnamon
1/4 cup melted margarine
1/2 tsp. salt
1/2 cup chopped almonds

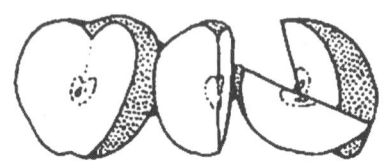

Crumble pieces of matzah into water and soak until soft (do not drown); squeeze out the excess moisture. Beat the eggs. Add sugar, salt and cinnamon, beating till well-blended. Stir crumbled *matzahs,* raisins, almonds, apples and orange rind into the egg mixture.

Turn it all into well-greased 1–1/2 quart casserole. Sprinkle more cinnamon and sugar and pour the melted margarine on top.

Bake at 350° for about 45 minutes, until firm and nicely brown. Serves 6–8.

5. MATZAH STUFFING
This is made the same way as regular bread stuffing, only use crumbled *matzah* and wet it down, squeezing out excess moisture. It can be made inside or outside the cavity of the roaster or turkey. Add some of the pan juices for flavoring if you make the stuffing in a casserole.

6. CARROT TZIMMES
Tzimmes is a word that means, well, a big to-do, as in "It's only a little scratch on the fender; don't make such a big *tzimmes* out of it."

A carrot *tzimmes* is a sweet concoction served alongside the main dish.

1–1/2 lb. carrots	6 Tbls. brown sugar
3 Tbls. margarine	1/2 tsp. cinnamon
1/2 tsp. salt	1/4 tsp. cloves
1 cup water	1 Tbls. lemon juice
1/2 cup raisins	Grated peel of one orange
1 cup prunes (pitted)	2 Tbls. honey

Peel and slice the carrot into 1/8"
slices. Melt margarine in a medium large
saucepan and sauté the carrots for 5 minutes.
Add the sugar and water and bring to a
boil. Stir in the remaining ingredients and
simmer, covered for 2 hours.

After 2 hours, remove the cover and
cook 20 minutes more. The *tzimmes* should
be moist but not too soupy. Serves 8.

7. SPONGE CAKE
(there are also mixes for this that you can buy)

6 egg yolks	6 egg whites
1-1/4 cups sugar	1/4 tsp. salt
2 tsp. lemon juice	1/4 cup potato flour
1 tsp. grated lemon rind	1/2 cup *matzah* meal

Almost all Passover baking recipes begin by telling you to
separate 6 eggs; that's because you can't use any leavening agent
for helping the cake to rise. Instead you whip the whites into a
frenzy as you'll see here. (This is definitely *not* a holiday for those
who have sworn off eggs.)

Beat the egg yolks; gradually add the sugar. Beat them together
until thick and light in color. Stir in the lemon juice and rind.

Beat the egg whites (see?) and salt until stiff but not dry. Pile
them on top of the egg white mixture. Sift the potato flour and
matzah meal over it all and fold together *very carefully.*

Turn the mixture into an ungreased 10-inch tube pan and
bake at 325° for 50 minutes to an hour, or until lightly browned
and free from the sides of the pan. Invert and then let cool.

*(Note: because of the tenuous nature of the rising of
baked goods at Passover, we strongly suggest that
you do not allow toddlers to play "marching band"
anywhere near the oven during the baking process.)*

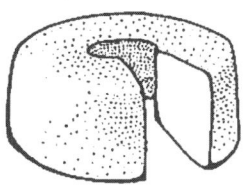

Serves 8–12, depending on the size of your pieces!

Dayenu
It Would Have Been Sufficient
דינו

dz- da- ye-nu   da-   ye- nu da-ye- nu   ye- nu da-ye-nu.

If God had merely rescued us from Egypt, Dayenu, It would have been sufficient.

(Other verses:)

> Ilu notan notan lonu,
> Notan lonu et ha *Torah,*
> Notan lonu et ha *Torah,*
> *Dayenu!* (sing chorus)

If God would have merely given us the Law (the Scriptures), Dayenu, it would have been sufficient.

> Ilu notan notan lonu,
> Notan lonu et Yeshua
> Notan lonu et Yeshua,
> *Dayenu!* (sing chorus)

God has given us Yeshua the Messiah, and he is sufficient!

Lashanah Haba'ah bi Yerushalayim, *final measures*

Eliyahu HaNavi
Elijah the Prophet
אליהו הנביא

May the prophet Elijah come soon, in our time, with the Messiah, son of David.

Lashanah Haba'ah bi Yerushalayim
Next Year in Jerusalem
לשנה הבאה בירושלים

Continued on page 17

The
Messianic
Passover
Seder

Preparation Guide

ISBN 978-1-880226-24-7

Lederer Books
a division of
MESSIANIC JEWISH PUBLISHERS
www.messianicjewish.net

9 781880 226247

50399 >